SPIROGLYPHICS. | MUSIC ICONS

Thunder Bay Press
An imprint of Printers Row Publishing Group
10350 Barnes Canyon Road, Suite 100, San Diego, CA 92121
www.thunderbaybooks.com

Printers Row Publishing Group is a division of
Readerlink Distribution Services, LLC.

Thunder Bay Press is a registered trademark
of Readerlink Distribution Services, LLC.

All notations of errors or omissions should be addressed to
Thunder Bay Press, Editorial Department, at the above address.

All other correspondence (author inquiries, permissions)
concerning the content of this book should be addressed
to The Ilex Press, Carmelite House, 50 Victoria Embankment,
London, EC4Y 0DZ, UK.

For Ilex:
Publisher: Roly Allen
Editorial Director: Zara Larcombe
Managing Specialist Editor: Frank Gallaugher
Editor: Rachel Silverlight
Admin Assistant: Stephanie Hetherington
Art Director: Julie Weir
Puzzle Testing: Emma Suttey at M Made, Rosanna Silverlight
Senior Production Manager: Peter Hunt

For Thunder Bay:
Publisher: Peter Norton
Associate Publisher: Ana Parker
Publishing/Editorial Team: April Farr, Kelly Larsen, Kathryn C. Dalby
Editorial Team: JoAnn Padgett, Melinda Allman, Traci Douglas

ISBN: 978-1-68412-093-2

Printed in China

23 22 21 20 19 4 5 6 7 8

SPIROGLYPHICS® | MUSIC ICONS

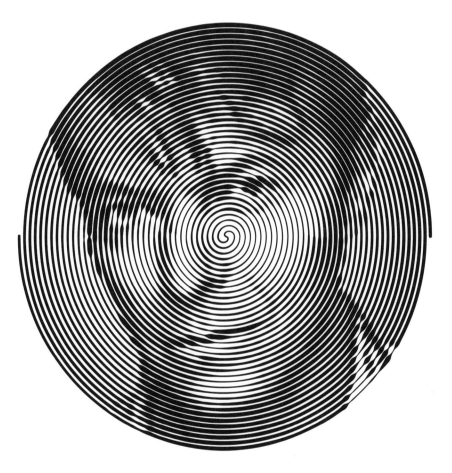

THOMAS PAVITTE

AUTHOR OF THE
BEST-SELLING
QUERKLES AND
1000 DOT-TO-DOT
BOOK SERIES

THUNDER BAY
P·R·E·S·S
San Diego, California

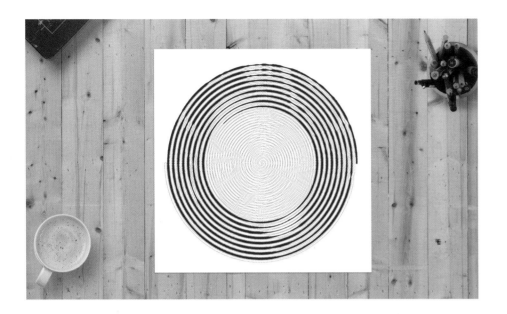

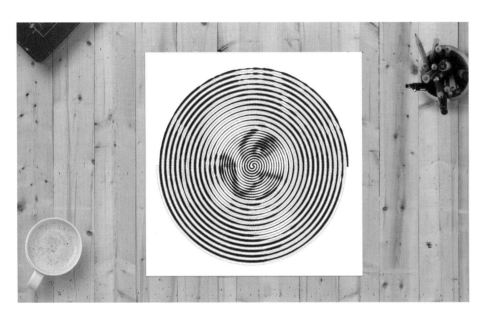

COLOR, CREATE, AND REVEAL WITH AMAZING SPIROGLYPHICS®

At first glance, spiroglyphics appear to be nothing but simple spirals. But if you look a little closer you'll see that the spiroglyphics are in fact two spirals, joined at the middle, and varying subtly in width as they wind to the center. It's only when you pick up a pen and start to color them that they come alive…

Choose one end of the spiral to begin (it doesn't matter which), and start coloring in. You can work quickly—the lines are more forgiving than you think, so don't worry if you're not the neatest at coloring. Just enjoy the process of revealing the iconic musician hidden in the spirals. When you reach the center on the first spiral, take a step back and have a look. Can you work out who it is yet? Then, working back to the outside, you'll see the details beginning to appear, like magic! And the result? Stand back to get the full effect—how did you do that with just a pen and a spiral?

The simplest way to complete the spiroglyphics is with a black felt-tip pen, but there are endless numbers of fun variations you can try. Here are some ideas:

• Color in the white, background spiral too. Try out different color combinations—how about contrasting colors, or light and dark shades of a single color? (Do some experiments before you begin!)

• Color in just the face, or the background around the face. Could you use pencils to color the face in flesh tones? How about a pop-art look?

• Divide the spiroglyphic into sections, using pencil, before you begin, and use a different color on each section. You can simply split the puzzle in half, or get creative with different shapes…

• Choose a number of rings to complete in one color, then switch to another color. How many colors do you want to use? What colors make the most striking combinations?

• If you want to take the person in the puzzle for your inspiration, you can flip to the back of the book, where you'll find all the completed puzzles in the order they appear, and find out who you're about to color.

TWEET IT, POST IT, PUT IT ON YOUR WALL. TIME TO START YOUR COLLECTION.

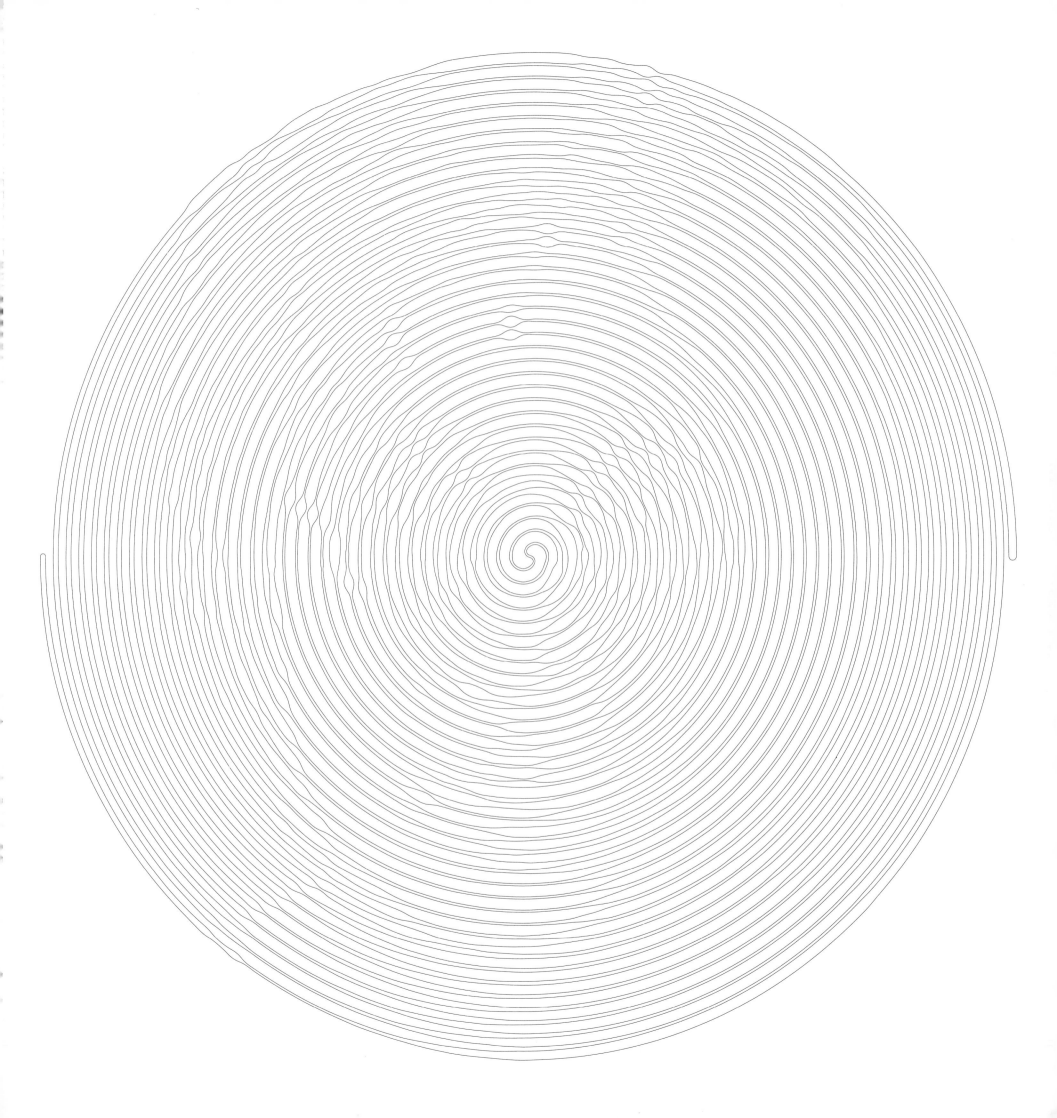

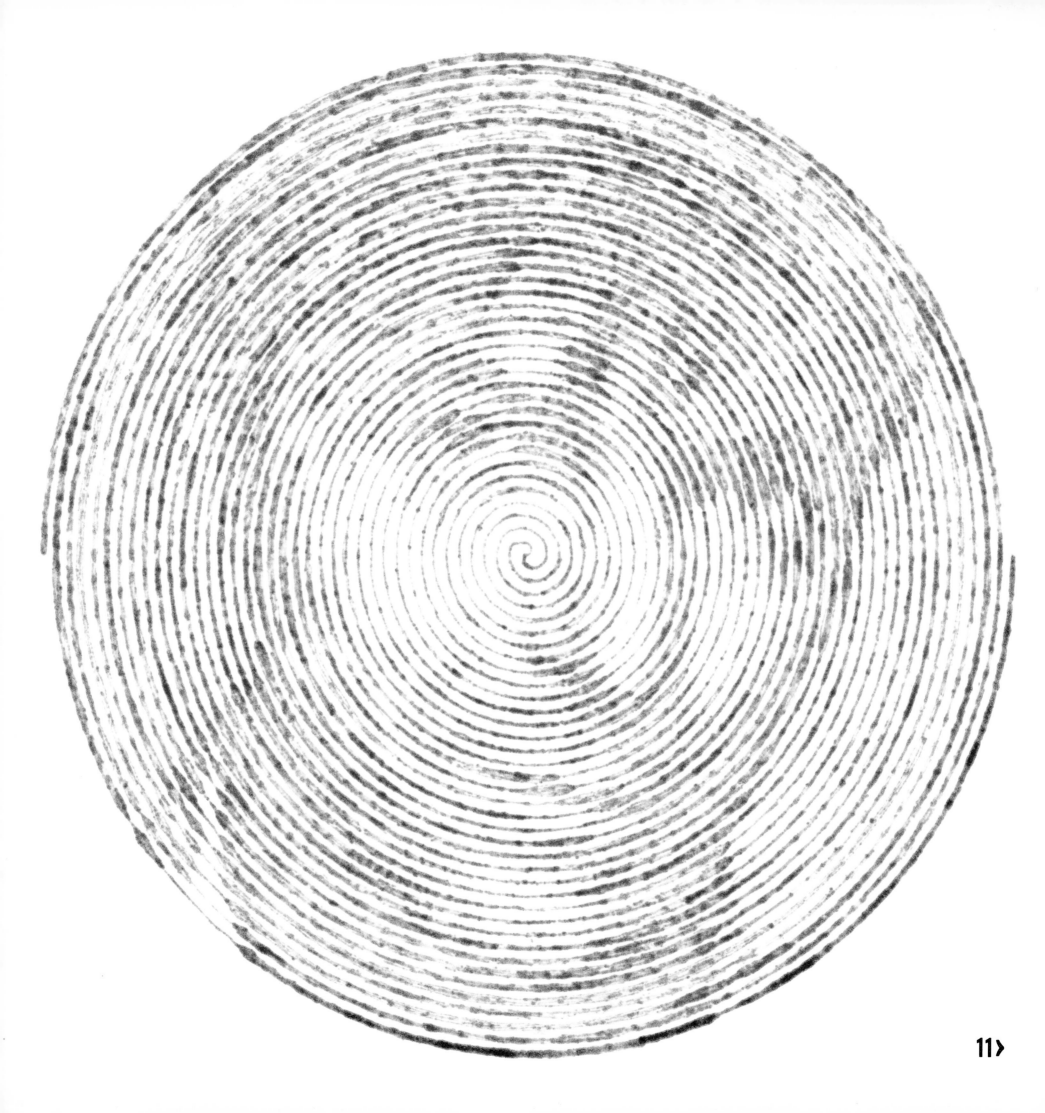

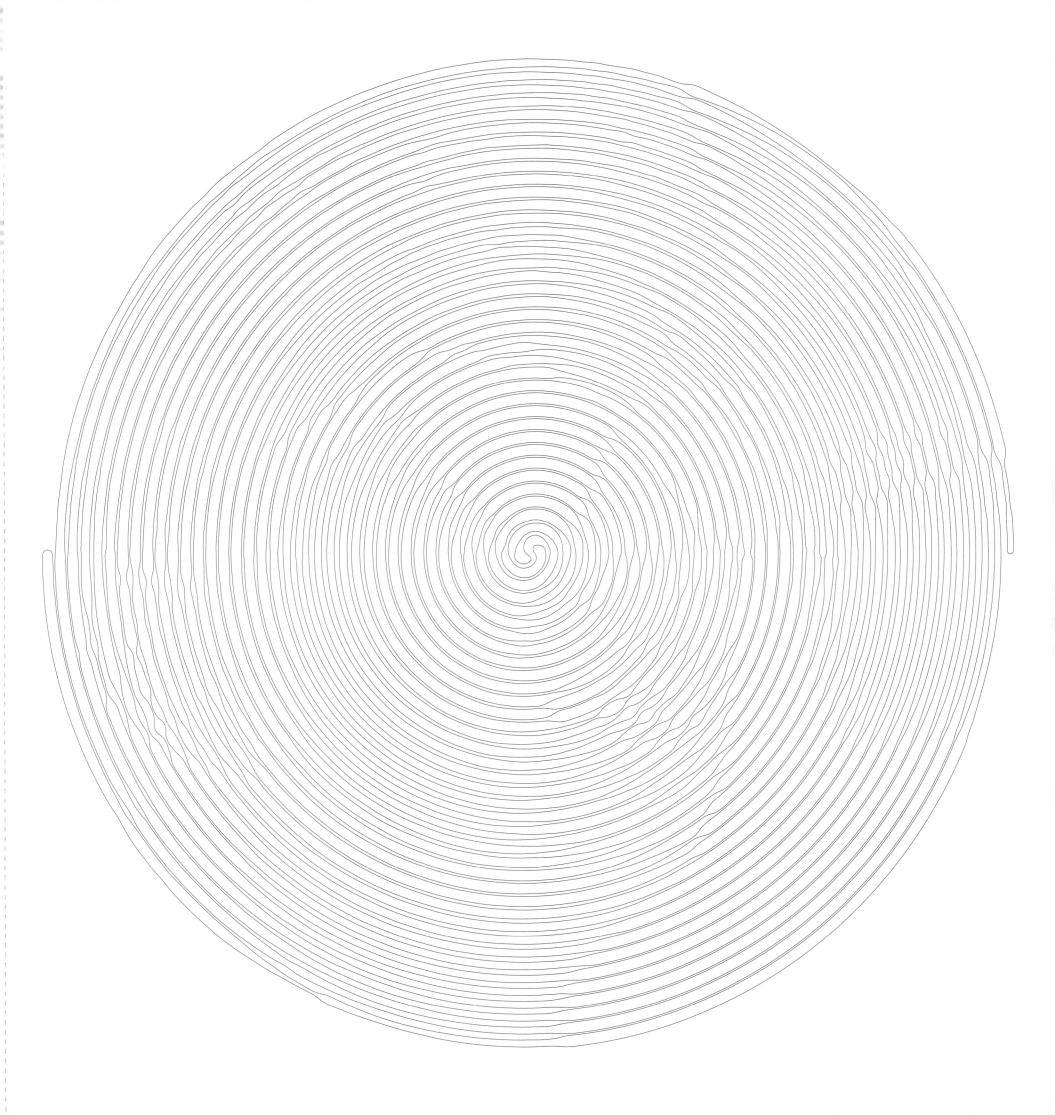

ACKNOWLEDGMENTS

In this age of digital technology it's amazing to think that vinyl records are still such a popular way of playing music. For me the beauty of vinyl is its simplicity—just a groove and a needle producing sound. *Spiroglyphics* is my interpretation of this simple concept and it has been an absolute joy to create my first book featuring some of my all-time favorite artists.

PICTURE CREDITS

Madonna: Julian Wasser/Liaison; Jimi Hendrix: Photoshot/Getty Images; Mick Jagger: Keystone Features/Getty Images; Beyoncé: Ray Amati/Getty Images; John Lennon: Evan Agostini/Liaison; Elvis Presley: Michael Ochs Archives/Getty Images; Prince: Ron Galella, Ltd./WireImage; Janis Joplin: David Gahr/Getty Images; Bob Marley: Michael Ochs Archives/Getty Images; David Bowie: Terry O'Neill/ Getty Images; Debbie Harry: Anthony Barboza/Getty Images; Tina Turner: Ron Galella, Ltd./WireImage; Axl Rose: Michael Putland/Getty Images; Amy Winehouse: Dan Kitwood/Getty Images; Kurt Cobain: Frank Micelotta/Getty Images; Bob Dylan: Michael Ochs Archives/Getty Images; Stevie Nicks: Michael Ochs Archives/Stringer/Getty Images; Stevie Wonder: Rob Verhorst/Redferns; Elton John: Michael Putland/Getty Images; Michael Jackson: Time Life Pictures/DMI/The LIFE Picture Collection/Getty Images